Love is...

Bob Christopher

Love is…

ISBN-10: 1931899371

ISBN-13: 978-1-931899-37-6

Published by Basic Gospel Inc.

For my wife, Jeanna…
Thank you for loving me.

Contents

Introduction

Christianity is filled with people who think they have it all together. They've figured it all out and can speak to every issue and problem. At least, that is what they think. I was one of those guys.

I couldn't understand why other Christians didn't have it together like me. All the dots were connected in my mind and everything about the Christian life made sense. Yes, call me naïve, idealistic or even unrealistic. You might even want to chuckle. I certainly do when I look back at those days.

I did think I had it all together. And I truly believed I was more than qualified to speak to the problems of the church. After all, I did have all the answers.

Mind you, I was in my early twenties at the time. I didn't have a lot of experience to speak of, but I did know what was wrong with the church. At least that is what I thought. Here was my analysis: "The church needs to love more." Brilliant, right? But here is what I meant. The church should be doing more to help people in need. Every chance I got, I railed about what I perceived to be the church's lack of vision and effort to help the poor and underprivileged in our community.

One day it dawned on me that I should stop talking about the problem and get about the business of loving those in need. Boy was I in for a shock. I quickly found out that I knew very little if anything about love.

I volunteered to be a Big Brother. The

coordinator paired me with Floyd. Floyd was 43 years of age with the mental capacity of a second grader. He lived in a group home and spent most of his days at the local community center along with many other mentally challenged citizens. I met Floyd for the first time at this community center.

At first glance, I could tell there was something special about him. I really wanted to make a difference in his life.

I asked Floyd what he wanted to do the next time we got together. Without hesitation, he blurted out, "Bob, I want to go to Six Flags." I wasn't expecting this response, but I thought it would be great fun for the two of us. We picked a date. As I left, I looked back and saw Floyd grinning from ear to ear.

As the day drew closer, something strange started happening in me. I found myself not wanting to go. As a matter of fact, I was dreading taking Floyd to Six Flags. I didn't understand why I felt this way at first. It was going to be a fun outing, and I knew Floyd would have the time of his life. But…

What would people think of me? Would they laugh at me, or make fun of me? Would I ever live it down with my friends that I went to Six Flags with a 43 year old mentally challenged "Little Brother?"

I knew I couldn't back out. The day meant too much to Floyd.

To my delight, I awoke that Saturday morning to the sound of rain. The forecast called for heavy rains throughout the entire day. I called Floyd with the bad news, but I promised I would take him the following Saturday.

That next Saturday was beautiful. When I picked up Floyd, he had a big smile on his face. He was ready to experience the best day of his life.

The Log Jamboree was the first ride of the day. The line was long, about a 45 minute wait. Approaching our turn, we marched up several steps and then crossed over a short bridge. While standing on the bridge, we watched those ahead of us taking off on their "white–water" adventure. After a few minutes, we walked down steps on the other side of the bridge and loaded into our log.

The attendant released the lever and off we went, around the bend and under the bridge. Right as we got to the bridge, Floyd ripped off his shirt and raised his hands to the sky. His spontaneous show of emotion turned the heads of onlookers. I felt a thousand pairs of eyes staring right at us. I wanted to hide under the seat. As I looked back, people were pointing and laughing. Floyd was joyfully oblivious to the jeers and sneers. I, however, felt every one.

Lunch was more of the same. Floyd wanted a hamburger with French fries. We got our food and searched for a table. The only one available was right next to the park's main walkway. Of course we were there on one of the most crowded days of the year. Floyd piled on the ketchup and mustard. He opened his mouth wide and then chomped down on that juicy burger. Ketchup and mustard flew everywhere to the amusement of onlookers. And with each bite Floyd took, a steady stream spewed down his chin and onto his shirt.

I lowered my head and waited for Floyd to finish. He ate every bite. What he did leave was prominently displayed on his shirt. He cleaned up with little help from me, and then off we went to conquer the rest of the park.

At four that afternoon, Floyd was spent. He had given his all and experienced fun beyond his wildest imagination. But he was ready to go home. I was ready to go home, too. Protecting my fragile self-image had taken its toll on me.

As we were walking toward the gate to leave, Floyd put his arm around me, pulled me close and said, "Bob, I love you!"

My chin started to quiver. I fought to hold back the tears. I knew he genuinely meant it, but his words crushed me.

This day was supposed to be about Floyd, but all I could think about was good old me. Floyd didn't know what was going on inside my heart and mind. For him, the day was monumental. He told his friends at the group home that it was the best day of his life. And it should have been the best day of my life.

It turned out to be one of the most painful. The day exposed my insecurities and fears. Floyd's words brought them into razor sharp focus. His words also let me know that I knew very little, if anything, about the love of God.

I wanted to love people the way Jesus did, but that day I failed miserably. It took several years to pinpoint the problem. Finally, it hit me like a ton of bricks: *I couldn't love like Jesus because I didn't know how He loved me.*

Maybe, you've had a similar experience. Maybe you know the frustration of trying to love someone with the love of God only to end up totally concerned with your own issues. If that is the case, I invite you to step back and take a fresh look at the definition of love. What the Bible tells us about the love of God is life-changing. That's what we will examine in this book.

Let me say up front. God wants you to know and experience His love more than anything else in life. So much so, He moved Paul to pen this incredible prayer:

> *I pray that out of his glorious riches*
> *He may strengthen you with power*
> *through His Spirit in your inner being,*
> *so that Christ may dwell in your hearts*
> *through faith. And I pray that you, being*
> *rooted and established in love, may have*
> *power, together with all the saints, to*

grasp how wide and long and high and deep is the love of Christ, and to know this love that surpasses knowledge—that you may be filled to the measure of all the fullness of God. (Ephesians 3:16-19)

This is my prayer for you. I pray you will adopt it as your personal prayer. I guarantee this is a prayer God will answer in ways that far exceed anything you could "ask or imagine" (Ephesians 3:20).

God Is...

Let's begin with one of my favorite passages in the Bible, 1 John 4:7, 8. The Apostle John had this to say about love: "Dear friends, let us love one another, for love comes from God. Everyone who loves has been born of God and knows God. Whoever does not love does not know God, because God is love." Let those last three words sink in.

God is love. Yes, He is just, sovereign, and

omniscient, as the Bible declares, but His essence is love. According to this passage, the people who love others do so because they know that God is love. The reason is twofold. First, they've been born of God. And second, they know God. They know He is love and that He is the source of love. But what about those people who do not love? John answers very clearly. They do not love because they do not know God.

Maybe you once thought God was mean and judgmental. Or that He was demanding, exacting perfection from you. Maybe you pictured Him as an ogre, always angry with you, or disgusted with you. That's what sin makes us think about Him. But none of this is true. He is not like that at all.

He is love. Jesus makes this incredible truth known to us through His death, burial and resurrection. Each aspect of the Gospel story shouts the truth – God is love. That's what people respond to. This response of faith is a sign of new birth, that a person has been born of God. It's what John describes as receiving Jesus Christ.

If you've never received Jesus Christ, I encourage you to do so right now. Here is a wonderful passage from the Gospel of John. "Yet to all who received Him, to those who believed in His name, He gave the right to become children of God—children born not of natural descent, nor of human decision or a husband's will, but born of God" (John 1:12, 13). This is the first step to knowing that God is love. Jesus made this clear. "I tell you the truth, no one can see the kingdom of God unless he is born again" (John 3:3).

For the rest of this book, we are going to explore what God's love looks like and how He expresses that love toward us.

The word for love in the Bible is *agape,* and it is a word that signifies action. The Complete Word Study Dictionary defines *agape* as God's willful direction toward man. We think of love as a feeling. That's not the case. It's an action. God does for us what is best for us.

This action of love that God directs toward us is best seen in 1 Corinthians 13:4-7:

> *Love is patient, love is kind, it does not envy, it does not boast, it is not proud, it is not rude, it is not self-seeking, love is not easily angered, it keeps no record of wrongs. Love does not delight in evil but rejoices with the truth, it always protects, it always trusts, it always hopes, it always perseveres. Love never fails.*

This is the definition of love. Here is what Paul means. God is patient with you. He is kind to you. In relation to you, He does not envy or boast. God is not proud, or rude, or self-seeking. God is not easily angered with you, nor does He keep records of your wrongs. God does not delight in evil but rejoices with the truth. God always protects. He always trusts. He always hopes. He always perseveres. God never fails you.

For the rest of this book, we will take a close look at the love God has lavished on us, and we'll consider how His love impacts our daily lives. We'll find that we can never know it all when it comes to the love of God. Just when we think we've got it, His love will expand a little higher, a little deeper, a little wider and a little longer. That is God's love. It is who He is, and as we continue to grow in our relationship with Him, we will learn to know His love even more.

Before we dive in, an observation. It is impossible to know and experience the love of God through law, or any other system of rules and regulations. Try as hard as we may, we can never do enough to earn God's love and acceptance. We don't have what it takes. To our failed attempts, the law tells us we are guilty and deserve punishment. Yet, we keep trying. I call this an Old Covenant mindset. It leads to nothing but fear in our hearts. Paul knew all about this old covenant way of life. Here is what he said about it:

Therefore, since we have such a hope, we are very bold. We are not like Moses, who would put a veil over his face to keep the Israelites from gazing at it while the radiance was fading away. But their minds were made dull, for to this day the same veil remains when the old covenant is read. It has not been removed, because only in Christ is it taken away. Even to this day when Moses is read, a veil covers their hearts. But whenever anyone turns to the Lord, the veil is taken away. Now the Lord is the Spirit, and where the Spirit of the Lord is, there is freedom. And we, who with unveiled faces all reflect the Lord's glory, are being transformed into His likeness with ever-increasing glory, which comes from the Lord, who is the Spirit. (2 Corinthians 3:12-18)

When we allow religious rules and regulations to define our relationship to God, our minds are made dull and a veil covers our hearts. We can't see the love of God. Through this lens, all we see is fear and punishment. When we look to Christ, the veil is taken away and we can see clearly. Here is the good news. As believers, we do not live by the Old Covenant. We live in the New Covenant. In this New Covenant, God has forgiven our sins, opened the way into His presence, given us assurance of salvation, and has made us new on the inside. This is a covenant of love and grace, not one of condemnation and punishment. Christ made this New Covenant effective through His death on the cross. He fulfilled the Old, so that we could live in the New.

As you read through this book, I ask you to do so looking through the lens of the New Covenant. It is the New Covenant that brings Jesus into laser sharp focus and tells us that God is love.

Love is Patient
Chapter 1

"Lord, give me some patience…and give it to me now!" For us, patience is like a battery that constantly needs recharged. Even then, what we call patience is often simply "putting up" with a situation. We feel frustrated and angry, gritting our teeth, tensing our necks, hoping the situation will go away before our patience completely runs out. On the freeway, it's gone in less than a second. God's patience, on the other hand, never has to be recharged. It never has to be plugged in. His patience is part of His nature, part of who He is, which means He is always patient with us.

Paul's word choice emphasizes this wonderful point. Sometimes when we think of patience, we think more in terms of patience within adverse circumstances. The Bible does speak to this kind of patience. For example, Paul, knowing the trials and tribulations the Colossian Christians would face, prayed that God would strengthen them so that they might have "great endurance and patience" (Colossians 1:11). However, 1 Corinthians 13 speaks specifically about patience toward people.

The Greek word for patience is composed of two specific words, one is *makros*, meaning long; the other is *thumos,* meaning anger or wrath. When joined together, *makrothemeo* means long-suffering, as opposed to being quick to anger. To say that love is patient means that God suffers long with us. And He is doing so right now.

God acts this way toward us because He understands us. At some point in life, most of us have cried out, "God, You don't know how I feel!", or "God, You just don't understand!" But neither of these statements is true. He knows us and understands us better than we know ourselves. Consider these words about Jesus from the writer of Hebrews: "For we do not have a high priest who is unable to sympathize with our weaknesses, but we have One who has been tempted in every way, just as we are—yet was without sin" (Hebrews 4:15). Jesus knows us best. He knows what's going on in our hearts and in our minds. He knows our weaknesses, our struggles, our trials and tribulations. He knows that sin lives in our flesh and that we are subject to the temptations of the world. He knows we can do nothing of value apart from Him. He understands us, and He chooses patience over anger and wrath.

This is where we fall short. We don't even understand ourselves, much less others. We do not have the ability to peer into someone else's mind to know what is going on with them. This makes it difficult at best for us to exercise patience with others. Consider the Apostle Paul.

He did not understand why he did the things he did not want to do, or why he couldn't do the things he wanted to do. He didn't understand himself at all. Before he met Jesus on the road to Damascus, he certainly didn't understand why his fellow Jewish brothers would want anything to do with this Jesus guy. It angered him when any of his Jewish comrades left Judaism to follow who he thought was nothing more than a renegade. His anger turned him into "…a blasphemer and a persecutor and a violent man" (1 Timothy 1:12-13).

In his mind, Paul was doing God a favor by persecuting those who had named the name of Christ. He thought he was ridding the world of a rising sect that was leading people astray. He perceived his violence as righteous indignation. Those believers who were the victims of Paul's wrath had to wonder, "God, why are you allowing Paul to do this to us?" God knew what He was doing and He had a plan for Paul. God suffered long with him to save him. As Paul wrote to his young son in the faith, "…I was shown mercy so that in the worst of sinners Christ Jesus might display His *unlimited* patience as an example for those who would believe on Him and receive eternal life" (I Timothy 1:14-15). God's patience had a purpose for Paul. And His patience has a purpose for you.

The way God displayed His unlimited patience toward Paul is nothing less than astonishing. Paul, then known as Saul, stood with the Sanhedrin listening to Stephen's defense. Stephen told the history of God's dealings with Israel, and he concluded with this stark indictment, "You stiff-necked people! Your hearts and ears are still uncircumcised...you have received the law that was given through angels but have not obeyed it" (Acts 7:51-53). The leaders had heard enough. Stephen's words stirred up every ounce of anger in their hearts. They dragged Stephen outside of the city gates and stoned him. Saul watched with self-righteous approval. As soon as Stephen died, persecution swept through the church of Jerusalem. Saul went house to house dragging out believers to persecute them.

Later, with murderous words still on his tongue, Saul went to the leaders requesting letters to the synagogues in Damascus stating that if he found any following the Way he would take them as prisoners to Jerusalem. He started on his journey. Somewhere along the road, a bright light from heaven stopped him dead in his tracks. And then these words, "Paul why are you persecuting Me?" They must have cut him to the quick.

Paul wanted to be God's guy more than anything else. He aspired to be a leader among leaders. The irony is Paul actually believed he was God's guy and that his persecution of Christians was protecting God's good name. He was never more wrong, and according to law, his blasphemous acts deserved nothing less than what he approved for Stephen. The sentencing was much different, however. "Get up," Jesus said, "and go into the city, and you will be told what to do." Jesus was the offended party. He was the recipient of Paul's anger and fury. He could have punished Paul to the law's full extent. But no, it would not be so. Jesus bore the sins. He endured. Not many years prior, on a hill called Calvary, Jesus took Paul's punishment. Paul's sin issue was over. That day on the road to Damascus, Jesus showed Paul His unlimited patience, and extended mercy to the chief of sinners.

Jesus, through His long-suffering, turned this persecutor into a proclaimer of the Gospel and this blasphemer into one who would uphold the name of Jesus Christ. Is it any wonder that Paul began his definition of love with patience?

God is patient with us, "not wanting anyone to perish, but everyone to come to repentance" (2 Peter 3:9). "Bear in mind," Peter adds, "… our Lord's patience means salvation…" (vs. 15). Jesus died on the cross to remove the obstacle of sin once and for all, to usher us into a relation-ship with the living Father. That's the Gospel message. That's the New Covenant we live under today. In this New Covenant, we get to know God the Father personally and intimately through Jesus Christ. As we get to know Him, we'll see His patience in action time and time again.

Think about your life. What were you like as a person before you trusted Jesus Christ? I was a mess. I tried to be good, to be God's guy, but it never worked out. As hard as I tried, I could never win the battle over sin. I was expecting God's punishment at any time. But I received something much different – salvation. Certainly, God had the right to hurl every ounce of His anger toward me. But that's not God. He is patient, and He was patient with me. His patience meant eternal life for me.

I bet your story is much the same. No matter how far afield you got, God never gave up on you. He stuck with you through thick and thin. He let you get to a point where you could see who you really were apart from Him. His patience toward you enabled you to recognize you could not save yourself, and that you needed Him. And then one day, His love became real in your heart. His patience toward you meant your salvation.

Here is the good news. He is still pouring out His patience on you. He suffers long with the believer who struggles to rest in the completed work of Christ and as a result lives in fear that salvation is lost. He suffers long with the believer who is afraid she has committed the unpardonable sin because at some point in life she said an evil word about God or the Holy Spirit. He suffers long with those who struggle to break free from sinful habits and are weighed down with guilt and shame. We all have our issues. You know what your issue is. But let this truth sink in. Jesus never stops pouring His patience into your life.

And not only that, He promised to complete His work in us (Philippians 1:6). He's going to make that happen. Yes, we do dumb things along the way and we do mess up. We hurt each other's feelings. We get involved in things we shouldn't. But does God ever give up on us? No.

He suffers long to bring about His plan in each of our lives. He's promised to complete His work, and He's going to do it.

For a stunning example, we need only look to Israel and God's amazing patience toward this rebellious lot. In the Old Testament book of Exodus, when God met with Moses on top of the mountain He said this about Himself: "The compassionate and gracious God is slow to anger, abounding in love and faithfulness" (34:6). Nehemiah discovered this to be so. In speaking of his disobedient and "arrogant stiff-necked forefathers," he wrote, "You are a forgiving God, gracious and compassionate, slow to anger and abounding in love. Therefore You did not desert them" (9:16-17). Later, David, in Psalm 145:8, echoed the same truth: "The Lord is gracious and compassionate, slow to anger and rich in love." God did not desert the people of Israel. His love and faithfulness abounded to them.

He does not desert us, either. You may be crying out for His help or wisdom right now. It may seem like He isn't listening to your cries. Be assured that He is and that He is patiently working all the details of the situation together for your good. When the answer does come, count on it being better than anything you dreamed or imagined.

His patience doesn't end with you. God has put His Spirit in you so that you can be patient with others. It will only happen as you abide in Christ. He is the source, not you. Trust Him to work out patience in your life toward others. You'll know He is doing this. You'll look at people differently. You'll treat them with a sense of understanding. You won't be so quick to anger, or so quick to walk away. You'll reach out with a forgiving heart. When you see these things, you'll know it is because Jesus was and is patient with you. That's love in action.

Dear Heavenly Father,

Thank You for being slow to anger, for abounding in love and for never deserting us. At a specific point in time, You revealed to us the Good News: the death, burial and resurrection of Christ Jesus. You saved us. Thank You for your continued patience. You continue to work in our lives to complete the work You began. Help us to understand this. Give us a clear vision of what Your patience has meant and continues to mean in our day-to-day lives, so that we can extend Your patience to others. We thank You for patience, and we praise You that You direct patience toward us each and every day, in Christ's matchless name, Amen.

Love is Kind

Chapter 2

We look at others and say, "He's a kind person," or "She's kind." Kind people seem to like us. They smile a lot, and they pat us on the shoulder. When we are feeling kind, we might do something nice, make food for a sick person, or visit someone in the hospital. Society today calls these "random acts of kindness." If we hear a sermon on kindness, and we feel a little guilty, we may try harder to fill up our kindness bucket, but there are limits, depending on our mood and the person who is in our path. God's kindness, however, has no limit. His kindness is directed to the entire world. "For God so loved the world, He gave His one and only Son, that whoever believes in Him shall not perish but have eternal life." God's act of sending Jesus is kindness in action.

Kindness is in the list of the fruit of the Spirit (Galatians 5:22). It flows through our lives as we abide in the vine of Christ. Peter called it participating in His divine nature (2 Peter 1:4). But what exactly is kindness, and what does it look like?

The word *kind* in Webster's dictionary is defined as sympathetic, friendly, gentle, tender-hearted and generous. Isn't that how we think of the word *kind*? However, the word *kind* as it is used in I Corinthians 13:4, has a different definition. Here, *kind* comes from the Greek word which means useful. The Complete Word Study Dictionary defines *kind* as the willingness to help or assist, to be profitable to another. It's roll-up-your-sleeves and get into action to help someone in their time of need. We see this type of kindness most often after natural disasters hit.

This is what God does with us. He helps us in our time of need. He understands what needs to be done and He gets into action on our behalf. Since He is the only one who understands the deep need of our heart, His help is profitable, not sometimes, but always. In His loving kindness, He filled our greatest need through Jesus Christ.

What was that need? Paul hammered it home in Ephesians 2:1: "As for you, you were dead in transgression and sins…" We were dead spiritually and utterly helpless to save ourselves. There was nothing we could do. We were hopeless and helpless. God, however, could do something for us and He did. What He did we know as the Good News, "the power of God for the salvation of everyone who believes…" (Romans 1:16). God rolled up His sleeves and acted on our behalf. He did for us what was useful and beneficial. What could be more useful and beneficial than giving us life?

Many, however, show contempt for God's

kindness. The world champions the "I will" attitude. You may remember the movie titled *Invictus* (2009) that starred Matt Damon and Morgan Freeman. The story opens with the words of a poem. "I am the master of my fate: I am the captain of my soul." This is the attitude that says I don't need God's help. This is nothing new. This "I will" attitude was around before the world was ever created.

In Isaiah 14, Lucifer, the highest of created beings, was appointed to be a guardian. He was to help guard the creation that God brought into being. That wasn't good enough. Lucifer wanted more. In Isaiah 14:12-13, we read that Lucifer said, "*I will* raise my throne above the stars of God…*I will* make myself like the Most High…" Satan introduced this "I will" attitude into the world when he deceived Adam and Eve. It's the attitude that condemns weakness and mocks dependence on God. We know it as pride. Love reaches out to help others in kindness. Pride responds, "I don't need help. I can do it on my own." That's not true. We do need help. Recognizing this truth frees us to respond to the kindness God extends to us in the person of Jesus Christ, the kindness, as Paul wrote, that leads us to repentance.

Paul amplifies this idea in Titus 3:3: "At one time we too were foolish, disobedient, deceived and enslaved by all kinds of passions and pleasure. We lived in malice and envy, being hated and hating one another. But when the kindness and love of God our Savior appeared, He saved us, not because of righteous things we had done, but because of His mercy." Based on this passage, it's a foolish notion to think we can "I will" ourselves to salvation. Satan's lie will never work.

This isn't a passage that paints the kindness of God as just a warm fuzzy feeling. No, God's kindness is an action filled with energy and effect. God's kindness saves us "through the washing of rebirth and renewal by the Holy Spirit whom He poured out on us generously through Jesus Christ our Savior so that having been justified by His grace we might become heirs having the hope of eternal life" (Titus 3:4, 5).

We were foolish and disobedient. We believed we could make it on our own, that God's help was unnecessary. The reality is that we were dead in sin. God in his mercy showed us our true condition so that we could humbly receive His kindness. Only God can save us from sin and death and make us new. In the Gospel, we see that God was willing to do something profitable for us that we could not do for ourselves. He did it through the washing of rebirth, the regeneration of these dead spirits of ours, and the renewal of the Holy Spirit.

God has come to live inside of you. Paul described this as "Christ in you, the hope of glory" (Colossians 1:27). This is the result of God's kindness.

In Ephesians 2:4, we are told, that "…because of His great love for us, God, who is rich in mercy made us alive with Christ even when we were dead in transgressions—it is by grace you have been saved." What is salvation? It is being made alive with Christ Jesus. Salvation is much more than forgiveness. Yes, we needed forgiveness. But our deepest need was life. So what did God do? He "raised us up with Christ and seated us with Him in the heavenly realms in Christ Jesus, in order that in the coming ages He might show the incomparable riches of His grace, expressed in His kindness to us in Christ Jesus. For it is by grace you have been saved, though faith, and this not from yourselves, it is the gift of God—not by works, so that no one can boast" (Eph. 2:6-9).

This gift of God is truly an act of kindness. We were helpless and hopeless, so there is nothing to boast about on our part. Jeremiah the prophet put it this way, "Let not the wise man boast of his wisdom or the strong man boast of his strength or the rich man boast of his riches" (Jer.9:23). Wisdom, strength and riches are wonderful to have. But are any of these things useful for salvation? Are any of these profitable for giving us life, or raising us from spiritual death? Absolutely not. We can be as wise as Solomon and still be dead in sin. We can be as strong as Samson and still be dead in sin. We can be as rich as King David and still be dead in sin. None of those are profitable for salvation. Jeremiah goes on to say in verse 24, "But let him who boasts boast about this: that he understands and knows Me, that I am the Lord, who exercises kindness, justice and righteousness on earth, for in these I delight."

God exercised justice by sending Jesus to be a sin offering. He didn't sweep sin under a carpet; He didn't ignore it. He dealt with it justly. "For the wages of sin is death, but the gift of God is eternal life in Christ Jesus our Lord" (Romans 6:23). In 2 Corinthians 5:21, we are told "God made Him who had no sin to be sin for us, so that in Him we might become the righteousness of God." In that act that occurred 2000 years ago, He extended us His kindness. Our hearts should overflow with gratitude that we have received the most profitable gift.

Dear Heavenly Father,
Thank You for understanding our great-
est need and acting in kindness on our
behalf. You made us alive with Christ
and sent Your Spirit to live in us. Give
us hearts that praise You every day for
Your act of kindness to us. Then give
us hearts that long to extend that same
kindness to others. The world desper-
ately needs something that will be useful
and beneficial and profitable. The world
needs Christ. Work in us a willingness to
extend the kindness of Christ to others.
We thank You and praise You in Christ's
matchless name, Amen.

Love Does Not...
Chapter 3

Often writers use contrast to sharpen the focus on the themes of their work. Paul employed this style in his definition of love. After patience and kindness, two acts that constitute God's love, Paul listed eight actions that are not love. As a matter of fact, these eight actions really show us the nature of sin. If you know anything about God, you know that He does not envy, boast, or seek His own good. He is not proud or arrogant. He is not rude. Nor is He easily angered or provoked. God is none of these things and neither is His love. But when sin has its way with us, we see all of these negative and hurtful actions. Really, all the things that love is *not* are the very things we see most prominent in the world. And we don't have to look beyond our own lives to see these attitudes and actions up close and personal.

To help get a broader sense of what love does not do, consider the list of five different translations of 1 Corinthians 13:4-6a:

> *…It does not envy, it does not boast, it is not proud. It is not rude, it is not self-seeking, it is not easily angered, it keeps no record of wrongs. Love does not delight in evil…*(NIV)

> *… love does not envy or boast; it is not arrogant or rude. It does not insist on its own way; it is not irritable or resentful; does not rejoice in wrongdoing…*(ESV)

> *…is not jealous; love does not brag and is not arrogant, does not act unbe-*

comingly; it does not seek its own, is not provoked, does not take into account a wrong suffered, does not rejoice in un-righteousness...(NASB)

... Love is not jealous or boastful or proud or rude. It does not demand its own way. It is not irritable, and it keeps no record of being wronged. It does not rejoice about injustice...(NLT)

...charity envieth not; charity vaunteth not itself, is not puffed up, Doth not behave itself unseemly, seeketh not her own, is not easily provoked, thinketh no evil; Rejoiceth not in iniquity...(KJV)

As you can see, there is wide variation in these translations, giving a much deeper sense of the meaning of these words. We can more clearly understand all that love is not. But even more important, against this dark backdrop, we will see the love of God in vivid, life-changing detail.

Love Does Not Envy

You have a new car and I don't. You got the job and I didn't. I'm hot! The Greek word for envy is interesting because it's a word that means to be hot. Envy is inflammatory; it can simmer for years, or it can explode quickly. To envy is to feel discontent with others because of their advantages or possessions, to resent others who have something we desire. We're familiar with that, aren't we? My kids are in athletics. They have to try out to make certain teams. They do their best, and other kids do their best, but somebody is going to be a starter, and some-body is going to sit on the bench. The kids on the bench are envious of those who start. They get mad, hot over the whole situation. It's just the way things are. It's just the way we are.

Unlike us, envy is not a part of God's nature. After all, He spoke and the world came into be-ing. Colossians 1:17 tells us that "He is before all things, and in Him all things hold together." He's the one who makes this whole thing tick. God does not have to look at Bill Gates or Warren Buffett and say, "Wow, I wish I had their wealth. If I could just be Warren Buffett or Bill Gates for one day…" God is not envious of those guys. He's not resentful over what folks in the world have; He's not trying to get those things for Himself. He is perfectly content with who He is.

We're told in Acts that "The God who made the world and everything in it is the Lord of heaven and earth and does not live in temples built by hands, as if He needed anything, because He himself gives all men life and breath and everything else" (17:24-25). We like to build edifices and dedicate them to the Lord, and we think He's going to be so happy and so proud and pat us on the back and say, "Wow, this is wonderful!" But God doesn't live in temples built by hands. He lives in human beings.

Before knowing Jesus Christ, we were nothing but old dead stones. But all that changed the moment we came to Him by faith. He made us alive, and now we "as living stones are being built into a spiritual house…" (1 Peter 2:5). We are the temple, God's dwelling place.

This is for our good, not His. God doesn't need anything. Nothing at all. You and I, on the other hand, need everything. We are a needy bunch. That neediness breeds discontentment, which can make us envious of others. But God isn't needy at all. Why? He gives all men life and breath. Whatever we hold in our hands is a gift from Him.

In 2 Peter 1:3, Peter writes, "His divine power has given us everything we need for life and godliness…" It is not that God gives us some things, and if we work real hard, He'll give us other things, and then if we work even harder, He will give us more. At the moment He saved us, He gave us everything we need for life and godliness. Paul put it this way in Ephesians 1:3, "Praise be to God and the Father of our Lord Jesus Christ who has blessed us in the heavenly realms with every spiritual blessing in Christ."

How many spiritual blessings have we been given in Christ? Every spiritual blessing. We need to be anchored to this truth, so that we don't have to look out into the world to see if there's something we're lacking. There's not. Consider this question. Can you think of anything in this world that is greater than being named a child of God? In Christ, that is who you are. You are somebody, and you didn't even have to strive for it! You trusted in Jesus, and you were born again into the family of God. As His child, you are a joint heir with Jesus Christ. You've been ushered into this New Covenant, and you have every benefit that God has for you.

He doesn't give some believers more than others. We all have access to the throne of grace. We all are in relationship with the Lord Jesus Christ. We all have the gift of God's Spirit living inside of us. We can all say with confidence that He remembers our sins no more, that there is no more sacrifice for sin. These are the spiritual blessings we have been given in Christ Jesus. So why do we look into the world to see if there is something we are missing?

When we realize we have it all, we can actually say, "Lord, use me to minister to others so that others can see the love of God, and realize that all they are looking for is in Christ." We don't need to be envious. In Christ, we have it all.

Love Does Not Boast

Just as love does not envy, it also does not boast. The word *boast* in Greek, which is only used in 1 Corinthians 13:4, comes from a word that means braggart. Braggarts brag or boast. It's what they do. But not God, not love.

You probably know people who love to brag and boast. They talk about their accomplishments, and all the stuff they have, and who they know, as if they are special, superior to everyone else. They think more highly of themselves than they ought, as Paul would say. They make you feel "little" in their presence, as if you don't measure up. At least this is how they make me feel. How could you call that love? It's not.

The Bible calls it worldliness. John the Apostle wrote, "Do not love the world or anything in the world. If anyone loves the world, the love of the Father is not in him. For everything in the world, the cravings of sinful man, the lust of his eyes and *the boasting of what he has and does*, comes not from the Father but from the world" (I John 2:15-16). Boasting does not come from God. Here is the reason.

Boasting is nothing more than a lie. Think about it. Those who boast and brag think they are superior to everyone else. Is that true? They may have more stuff and greater accomplishments, but does that make them better than anyone else. Okay, I can't resist. They put on their pants one leg at a time just like you do. I bet you've heard that a time or two in your life. This has become cliché because it's true. Just because a person has more than someone else does not make him superior to that person. According to the Bible, "all have sinned and fall short of the glory of God" (Romans 3:23). We all stand as equals at the foot of the cross.

Those who boast put others down. They humiliate those who, in their opinion, do not measure up. This was happening in Corinth. The rich in Corinth looked at their wealth as a sign of God's approval. They despised the poor and would not associate with them, even at the Lord's Supper. Paul confronted this evil head on. "For who makes you different from anyone else? What do you have that you did not receive? And if you did receive it, why do you boast as though you did not?" (1 Corinthians 4:7).

Those who boast live in a "me" universe. They are self-centered to the max. The world revolves around them, or at least that's what they think. This jades the way they view others. Like I've said, they seem to live to put others down. The dignity of others is of no concern to these braggarts. Paul warns that this self-centered bragging will be one of the causes of trouble during the last days. His words are alarming: "People will be lovers of themselves, lovers of money, boastful, proud, abusive, disobedient to their parents, ungrateful, unholy, without love, unforgiving, slanderous, without self-control, brutal, not lovers of the good, treacherous, rash, conceited, lovers of pleasure rather than lovers of God—having a form of godliness but denying its power. Have nothing to do with them" (2 Timothy 3:2-5).

Aren't you glad that God is not like this, that He does not brag or boast? He could. He has much to boast about. He spoke, and the world came into existence. He conquered death. Who are we in comparison? Yet, He is mindful of us. I love what the writer of Hebrews had to say about Jesus: He is not ashamed to call us brothers. Jesus became one of us, was tempted like we are and tasted death so that we could become like Him. That's love, a love that does not brag or boast, but reaches out.

Yes, we are humbled in His presence, but we are never humiliated. We may feel that He is miles away, yet in grace He draws us near. In love, He calls us, sinners by birth, His own. This is God, the One who "…chose the lowly things of this world and the despised things—and the things that are not—to nullify the things that are, so that no one may boast before Him. It is because of Him that you are in Christ Jesus, who has become for us wisdom from God—that is, our righteousness, holiness and redemption. Therefore, as it is written: 'Let him who boasts boast in the Lord'" (1 Corinthians 1:28-31).

Love Is Not Proud

Is it any surprise that pride follows envy and boasting? The word *proud* in 1 Corinthians 13 means to be puffed up or inflated. A child's balloon is nothing until it is inflated. When inflated, it becomes something different; it's puffed up. Pride is having a puffed up attitude. Paul says in Philippians 2:7-8, "Your attitude should be the same as that of Christ Jesus: Who being in very nature God, did not consider equality with God something to be grasped, but made Himself nothing, taking the very nature of a servant, made in human likeness. And being found in appearance as a man, He humbled Himself and became obedient to death, even death on a cross." Jesus, who created the world, made Himself nothing, like us. He took the very nature of a servant, humbling Himself, becoming the opposite of "puffed up." God humbled Himself, allowing Himself to be nailed to a cross like a common criminal. If God envied us, if He were a braggart, or if He puffed Himself up with pride, He would have never become one of us.

Paul says in 1 Corinthians 8:1 that "knowledge puffs up, but love builds up." We humans tend to be proud of what we know, and we love to boast about it. With our knowledge, however, we can become stumbling blocks to others. This isn't God's nature. He knows everything. There is nothing that He does not know. Yet, He never belittles us for our lack of knowledge. We, on the other hand, are quick to use the things we know to puff us up and give us a feeling of importance. Spiritual knowledge seems to puff us up the most. We can quote Bible verses in such a manner that we make others feel like second class believers. This is not the way of love.

This pride causes great harm. It pits us against each other. Think how we fight over doctrinal issues: do we baptize by immersion or is sprinkling sufficient; are we predestined or do we have a choice; are we raptured before the tribulation or at Jesus' return? These are all important issues to wrestle with and seek answers for. We should be able to have civil conversations about all of these topics. We should, but we don't. Most of these conversations escalate quickly into fights. "I'm right!" "No, I'm right and I can't believe that you would be so stupid to believe such nonsense!" "I bet you are not even saved!" Pride in both parties is the cause of these and similar vitriolic battles. You can see them daily in many of the Christian internet chat forums.

Pride divides us. This is what was happening in Corinth and it is still happening today. There are so many divisions in Christianity it is hard to keep up with all of them. We follow this person, or that person. We do so to gain a sense of identity or purpose. We become proud over our beliefs and boast that we are following the right path, which means that everyone else is following the wrong path. We become proud over the spiritual work we do and think that anything else isn't quite as important. So we end up judging each other.

Pride blinds us to sin. The Corinthians got so puffed up about their freedom that they bragged about the sexual immorality that was happening within the body. They failed to see the dire consequences this caused for others. This can happen to us, as well.

We can also get so puffed up with pride that we shift our focus away from Christ to things that are ultimately meaningless. Paul put it this way: "Do not let anyone who delights in false

humility and the worship of angels disqualify
you for the prize. Such a person goes into great
detail about what he has seen, and his unspiritu-
al mind puffs him up with idle notions" (Colossians 2:18).

God isn't proud, and He doesn't get puffed
up by who He is or by what He knows. There
is no reason for us to get puffed up. Peter says,
"All of you clothe yourselves with humility
toward one another because God opposes the
proud but gives grace to the humble" (1 Peter
5:5). When the message of grace confronts a
proud heart, guess what happens? Rebellion
intensifies. As children, we sang the song "Jesus Loves Me." We had no trouble singing the
words "I am weak, but He is strong." Pride,
though, hates admitting weakness or neediness.
Doesn't the world hate weakness? The opposite
of pride, which is humility, says we can cast all
our cares upon Him because He cares for us (1
Peter 57). That's good news. Isn't it?

God has given us everything for life and

godliness. There is nothing else that we need. We try hard to make a name for ourselves, but there is nothing greater than saying, "I am a child of God." We don't have to strive to become somebody. When we trusted in Jesus, we were born again into the family of God. "Now if we are children," Paul says, "then we are heirs—heirs of God and co-heirs with Christ…" (Romans 8:17). Our inheritance in Christ is a gift of grace. All praise and thankfulness is to Him and Him alone.

Love Is Not Rude

Agape love flows toward us, without demand or expectation. It is purely unconditional, no strings attached at all. It has the power to touch us no matter how ugly, distorted, or sick we are on the inside. Love, in the person of Jesus Christ, is an action, forever moving forward, creating, transforming souls, giving life, loving the unlovely.

God's love reaches out. It turns the other

cheek. It reaches out and touches us when we are untouchable. It is Jesus, before it is too late, seeing deep inside the paralytic, past his frozen body, to his real need. Agape love says, "Take heart, son, your sins are forgiven" (Matthew 9:2). It is Jesus touching the eyes of the blind, touching the hand of a dying mother-in-law, washing the dirty feet of the disciples. It draws us to God Himself, touching our brokenness. Why? Because He loves us. He loves you, and He loves me.

So how can love be rude? It cannot. God is not rude. We can be. Rudeness can flow from our fleshly desires at any time, and it is not pretty. I wish I could say that I was never rude, but that would be a lie. Here is what I've learned. Whenever I act rudely toward Jeanna or the kids, it is usually a harsh, jeering comment that humiliates and embarrasses them. It makes them feel disgraced as people and tears them down. Those are horrible consequences, but that's rudeness. It totally disregards the feelings and worth of others.

Bible translations vary in uses of words to suggest rude behavior. For example, we find "unseemly" instead of "rude" in the *King James Version* and "unbecomingly," in the *American Standard Version*. The underlying Greek construction of all these words, though, suggests action. Love does not behave in an indecent, ugly or unbecoming manner. It is not morally offensive, obscene, disgusting or repulsive. Those actions are rooted in self, not in the needs of others. If you ever see an action that is indecent, guess what? You can immediately identify it as not being love.

God doesn't act unbecomingly toward us. He's always patient with us, always kind with us; His love doesn't offend our moral sensibilities. We can be rude with each other, we can blare our pride and prejudices in the faces of other people and justify ourselves in doing so. We can be rude with a tone of voice that is irritated, condescending, or spiteful. We can be rude with a sigh, the way we roll our eyes, or with the turn of our head. We can be rude when

we check our smart phones while we pretend
to listen to another person. All of these acts are
rude acts. They can be harsh. They hit hard and
fast. These acts of rudeness never heal or lift up;
they never renew. Rudeness is self-seeking, not
other seeking. But God is not like that.

And He certainly did not want us to be like
that toward each other either. Jesus encouraged
us to live by the Golden Rule: "Do to others as
you would have them do to you" (Luke 6:31).
No one wants to be treated rudely. No one wants
to experience humiliation and embarrassment.
If you know you don't want to be treated rudely,
you might be less likely to be rude to others.
Yet, we are still rude at times. Every time we
are, we miss the mark of love. That's why the
Bible keeps calling us to grow in grace and in
our knowledge of Christ Jesus. Knowing Him
changes us. He renews our minds and trans-
forms our character. He works in us to develop
hearts that trust Him. In this trust relationship,
love, God's love, is expressed through us. And
that love is not rude.

Love Is Not Self-Seeking

In the Greek, the underlying construction of self-seeking is also a verb. It is an action, a behavior. As fallen beings, we understand the idea of self. However, God does not seek Himself. He seeks us. He seeks the very best for us. God never asks the question "What's in it for me?" That is the question we ask. We meet somebody new and start wondering: What's in this relationship for me? How can it help my business? How can it help my social status? What can I gain? We ask ourselves those questions, don't we? The answers to these questions are important to us. And if we judge there is nothing in it for us, we move on.

That's not God's nature. He sent Jesus, not for His good, but for our good, so that we as forgiven people can enjoy a relationship with God. This is the New Covenant. It's why Jesus came to earth. As John wrote, God so loved the world that He sent Jesus. But what if love was self-seeking? Jesus would have never come to save us by offering Himself as the sacrifice for our sins.

In the Garden of Gethsemane, Jesus said, "Father, if You are willing take this cup from Me; yet, not My will but Yours be done" (Luke 22:42). There was an agony in His soul as He looked toward the suffering He was about to endure. The agony was such that He was sweating great drops of blood. Was there another way that man could be saved? Did He have to suffer death and endure the punishment for man's sins? He was there to do the will of His Father, but could it be achieved through another means? He knew the answer. The purchase price for man was the blood of the unblemished Lamb of God, His blood. Nothing less would do. The Psalmist declared this of Jesus: "Here I am – it is written about Me in the scroll—I have come to do Your will, O God" (40:7). In this crucible of agony, Jesus cried out, "Not My will, but Yours be done." Both in life and death, Jesus carried out the will of His Father, a will that was seeking after us.

In 1 Peter 4, the Apostle Peter wrote, "Therefore, since Christ suffered in His body, arm yourselves with the same attitude, because he who has suffered in his body is done with sin. As a result, he does not live the rest of his earthly life for evil human desires, but rather for the will of God" (1-2). How are we to live in this world today? According to Peter, we are not to live to fulfill our evil human desires, to seek our own, to look out for number one, or to live as if the world revolved around us. No, we are to live for the will of God. This is possible only as we understand and abide in the love of God.

You may be asking the question, "What is God's will for me?" Paul puts it this way, "… give thanks in all circumstances, for this is God's will for you in Christ Jesus" (I Thessalonians 5:18). God is the faithful one, and we can trust Him to see through our brokenness and renew us so that we can seek the good of others. He loves us that much. Jesus Christ sought us out to satisfy our souls. When we embrace all He has provided, we experience rest and contentment, and our self-seeking comes to an end.

Are you still seeking contentment? Does your soul still hunger and thirst. Let your search end in Christ. Through Him, you can actually live out His love in this world.

Love Is Not Easily Angered

I Corinthians 13 tells us that love is not easily angered. The word *easily* is not actually in the Greek manuscripts, and some translations, such as the *King James Version*, use the word *provoked* instead of anger, which seems to be a more appropriate word.

The Greek word for *provoke* in this verse means to sharpen, to exasperate or stir up. To provoke is to incite an action or feeling. Provocation happens in an instance. Think of poking a wasp's nest with a stick. There's quick action, isn't there? Anger is an instantaneous spark that flares. I know what this is. Every time I hear about one of our kids being mistreated at school, either by another student or by a teacher, I get provoked. I want to go do something about it. I think, "You can't treat my kid that way!" I get excited about it, and there are intense feelings that I want to live out. This is the way our flesh responds. We get provoked, and we want to take action.

Of all the Bible characters, Peter was the one who was the most easily provoked to action. Imagine being in the Garden of Gethsemane with Jesus the night before His crucifixion. Peter is there along with the other disciples. You hear noise and it's getting louder. You turn and see a crowd of soldiers and teachers of the law bursting in, shouting, carrying weapons and torches. Surprisingly, you notice Judas leading the way.

He marches up to Jesus and kisses Him on the cheek. A group of soldiers reach to grab Jesus and arrest Him. You look over at Peter. His face is turning red; the anger is building up and is soon to reach the tipping point. He brandishes his sword, and with a swift swing, he slices off the ear of the chief priest's servant (John 18:10). The fearful, chaotic scene provoked Peter to action. At that moment, he forgot everything the Lord had told him. Jesus did not commend Peter. He didn't say to him, "Wow! Thank you for helping me out." No, he rebuked Peter, saying, "Put your sword away! Shall I not drink the cup the Father has given Me?" (11).

Unlike us, God is not easily provoked. It is not in His character to be hasty or excitable, though He has plenty of reasons. Look at us. Aren't we a mess? We fail even when we are trying to be our holiest. I've been reading the Word of God, trying to soak up what it has to say and praying, "Lord open my heart and mind so I can see the wonders of Your love and Your majesty," and then it happens. Out of no where, a dirty thought races through my mind. Has this ever happened to you?

I am glad God is not easily provoked. If these things did provoke Him, there would be no one existing on this planet. He would squash us all like bugs. Thank God, He doesn't get provoked. Our sins don't send Him to angry retaliation against us.

In His last hours on earth, Jesus was insulted, spit upon, and beaten beyond recognition. He could have retaliated. But He didn't. He entrusted Himself to His Father.

The chief priests, teachers of the law and elders mocked Him saying, "He's the King of Israel! Let Him come down now from the cross, and we will believe in Him" (Matthew 27:42). The crowd would have cheered Him as a hero, applauding what He did, but we would still be lost and dead in our sins. Instead, Jesus offered reconciliation in the form of forgiveness. "He who knew no sin, became sin for us, so that in Him, we might become the righteousness of God" (2 Corinthians 5:21). Christianity, unlike every other religion, believes in a God who bears the burden of our sins on His own shoulders.

Love is not easily angered. Love reaches down to us in forgiveness and reconciliation. Isn't that good news?

Love Keeps No Record of Wrongs

Agape love is illogical in the eyes of the world. Grace does not make sense to the world. We want to keep a record of wrongs. We build spreadsheets in our minds, and on them we list all the harsh things people have said to us and all the injustices we have experienced. We keep these lists fresh, repeatedly bringing them out with our spouses and children. We can almost quote an event word for word that happened years ago.

We keep these lists because at some point we want to even the score. And it's not just the wrongs of others that we keep. We have a secret record of our own wrong doings. We even list all the things we could have done, or should have done. When we review our lists, we wonder when God is going to take His revenge on us. But God doesn't think this way. Keeping a record of wrongs is not the love of God. He has already paid the debt of sin in full. It is finished!

There is more to this phrase, however, than just record keeping. We see it through the various ways different translations render this verse. The *English Standard Version* (ESV), for example, reads "love is not resentful." The *King James* says, "Love thinks no evil." These look very different than the NIV rendering, "love keeps no record of wrongs." You may be thinking, "Which one is right, or more accurate?" Here is where English is at a disadvantage. The idea Paul is communicating is much bigger than our English language can convey in a single phrase. Looking at the different translations actually helps us get the full picture.

When a person is hurt or sinned against, all sorts of things start to happen. People can hurt us and hurt us deeply. The sad thing is that we can do the same to others. But when we get hurt by the actions of others, we take note. It's a video record that we store in our minds, a high definition, 3-D video, mind you. Every aspect of the event is stored in vivid detail. We know the who, what, when and how, and we give a lot of brain time to figuring out the why. All this opens the door for resentment to creep in and set up shop in our minds.

The writer of Hebrews issued a severe warning in regard to resentment and bitterness: "See to it that no one misses the grace of God and that no bitter root grows up to cause trouble and defile many" (Hebrews 12:15). Resentment is not content to merely stew. It wants to cause trouble. All kinds of evil thoughts begin racing through the mind, hatching a plan for revenge.

At a conference many years ago, I mentioned a heinous crime that was headline news of the day. I can't remember the details, but I do recall the reaction of the people in the group. The things they wanted to see happen to the criminal were worse than his crime. That is the way our minds work when bitterness is in the mix. An eye for and eye, and a tooth for a tooth is not enough. Once a plan for revenge is hatched, we wait for the perfect time, the perfect place for the pay back. And when the revenge comes, we tally the score. The record says that we are ahead, and the flesh is satisfied.

Evil acts toward others don't just happen. They begin in the mind. In God's mind there is no evil. He is love. As James wrote, God cannot be tempted with evil, nor does He tempt anyone with evil. No, "each one is tempted when, by his own evil desire, he is dragged away and enticed" (James 1:14). God is the source of all that is good in our lives. Every good and perfect gift comes from Him. Forgiveness of sins is one of those good and perfect gifts.

John wrote this: "I write to you, dear children, because your sins have been forgiven on account of His name" (1 John 2:12). Did you know that you are a forgiven person in Christ? God reconciled you to Himself in Christ, and He does not count your sins against you (2 Corinthians 5:19). Whenever you sin, God is not resentful, nor does He think evil. And that sin doesn't get recorded in God's books. That is the most wonderful news in all the word of God.

God's spreadsheet is empty. He does not keep a record of our wrongs.

Because of this, He gives us that ministry of reconciliation to go out into the world and tell others the good news that God does not count their sins against them. In the New Covenant, the covenant which we live in today, God says, "Their sins and lawless acts I will remember no more" (Hebrews 10:17). God isn't thinking about all the things we did wrong yesterday or today. He has already thought about them, and He sent Jesus to deal with them once and for all. The debt, our debt, was paid in full.

Love thinks no evil; love keeps no record of wrongs. God's Spirit continually points us to the love of God, giving our hearts a measure of peace. That's love. When we understand it, it melts our hearts, doesn't it? We think, Lord I can't believe it. I can't believe that You don't keep a record of my wrongs. That's the love of God in action.

Love Does Not Delight in Evil

Superman is one of our most beloved action heroes. He was introduced during a dark, sinister time in history. The Great Depression was ravaging America. Hitler was striking terror in Nazi Germany. Stalin's dreadful reign was wreaking havoc on Russian soil. Everywhere you looked, evil was winning. Americans needed hope.

The imaginations of two men from Cleveland offered Superman as a ray of hope. This super being with super powers would fight "the never ending battle for truth, justice and the American way." He would take a stand against the evil forces in the world and bring justice to those who were oppressed and down-trodden.

In the real world, love takes that stand. Jesus is the real hero. He does not delight in evil, but rejoices with the truth.

The word *evil* refers to those acts that are unjust. They are works of iniquity. Those who engage in these acts have no regard for God or man. They purposely suppress the truth to deceive and defraud others. Think of Judas Iscariot and Simon the Sorcerer. Both delighted in evil for their own sordid gains. Judas betrayed Jesus with a kiss. Thirty pieces of silver was the "reward for his evil" (Acts 1:18). Simon the Sorcerer tried to buy the gift of the Holy Spirit. Peter saw right through his façade: "For I see that you are full of bitterness and captive to sin" (Acts 8:23).

This type of evil persists today. Evil men are suppressing the truth, acting unjustly, and taking advantage of others. Bernie Madoff pocketed millions of dollars through an elaborate Ponzi scheme based on lies and deceit. Thousands of people invested their life savings and now have nothing. Oppressive governments take advantage of their citizens. Young girls are kidnapped and used for sex trafficking. God does not delight in these atrocities.

He takes a strong stand against the injustices of the world. Heaven declares His disapproval: "The wrath of God is being revealed from heaven against all the godlessness and wickedness of men who suppress the truth by their wickedness" (Romans 1:18). This word *wickedness* is the same word rendered *evil* in 1 Corinthians 13:6. People who are evil hide the truth. They keep others from seeing what is true and real. They lie and deceive, which is how they persuade others to participate in their evil schemes and godless activities.

This is nothing new. It all began in the garden. Satan started it with these four words: "Did God really say?" You know the story. Adam and Eve bought the lie. Satan defrauded their innocence and swept them up in his plan of destruction. Since that time, he has invested his efforts in keeping the truth from ever surfacing in the world. Why? The truth is dangerous to Satan's agenda. It sets people free. Truth opens up a window of love and grace and mercy to those who will respond, and Satan doesn't want that.

As Jesus said, Satan "was a murderer from the beginning, not holding to the truth, for there is no truth in him. When he lies, he speaks his native language, for he is a liar and the father of lies" (John 8:44). And there are those in this world who live to carry out Satan's desires – to kill, steal and destroy.

God does not sit back. Unlike Satan and his minions, He is not unjust. He does not lie. He does not suppress the truth because He is truth. He does not take advantage of us or oppress us. No, He extends His mercy and compassion. He brings truth to us in the person of Jesus Christ. He cleanses us of all unrighteousness. This is God. This is love, love that does not delight in evil, but rejoices with the truth.

———⟡———

Dear Heavenly Father,
Thank You that Your love never causes
us harm. Thank You that Your actions to-
ward us are always for our good. Sin has
messed this world up and has darkened
the hopes and dreams of so many. It has
brought harm and destruction. Thank
You that Your love is not like that. We are
so grateful that You sent Jesus into this
world so that we could see the full extent
of Your love toward us. In Jesus, we see
something different than what the world
offers, something that restores and lifts
us up. Help us to grow in Your love and
to learn by faith to express Your love
to others. In Christ's matchless name,
Amen.

———⟡———

Love Rejoices with the Truth
Chapter 4

Love does not rejoice with evil, but rejoices with the truth. This word *rejoice* as it relates to the truth is not the same word used in the first part of the verse. Rejoice conveys the idea of sharing in another person's joy, or to rejoice together. The story of Elizabeth, as told by Luke, exemplifies this type of joy. Elizabeth was old and barren, which was disgraceful to her. However, in her elderly years, she became pregnant. Her son was John the Baptist. When her neighbors and relatives found out "that the Lord had shown her mercy, they shared her joy" (Luke 1:58). They rejoiced with her. This is what love does.

In 2011, the Dallas Mavericks won the world championship in basketball. They beat the Miami Heat to take the title. No one expected them to win. But they won, and they won in a big way. To celebrate, the Maverick organization along with the city of Dallas planned a parade. Thousands of people garbed in Maverick attire lined the streets. These fans on that day felt the joy of the Maverick team. They shared in the victory those twelve players won. For the city of Dallas, it was a magical time of rejoicing. But this doesn't compare at all to the rejoicing that takes place when truth wins out in our lives.

In Luke 15, Jesus told his disciples a parable about a lost sheep. "Suppose one of you has 100 sheep and loses one of them? Does he not leave the 99 in the open country and go after the lost sheep until he finds it? And when he finds it, he joyfully puts it on his shoulders and goes home. Then he calls his friends and neighbors together and says, rejoice with me. I have found my lost sheep. And I tell you that in the same way, there will be more rejoicing in heaven over one sinner who repents than over 99 righteous persons who do not need to repent." This is the type of rejoicing packed in 1 Corinthians 13:6.

Think about the day you responded to the truth of the Gospel. This truth set you free from the law of sin and death. This truth made you alive together with Christ. This truth cleansed you of all unrighteousness and made you right with God. And according to Jesus, the work of truth in your life was cause for rejoicing in heaven. Your newfound joy was shared in the heavenly realms.

God did not delight in the fact that you were lost, that you were a slave to sin and death, and that you were subject to the ways of the world. He did not delight in the fact that Satan had a hold on you through his lies and deceits. In love, He sought you out and revealed the truth. Paul put it this way in his second letter to the Thessalonians: "But we ought always to thank God for you, brothers loved by the Lord, because from the beginning God chose you to be saved through the sanctifying work of the Spirit, through belief in the truth."

What happened when you believed the truth? Salvation! And Heaven rejoiced. The entire heavenly realm lined the streets to share in your joy. They rejoiced, because you were made alive in Jesus Christ. He called you to this through the gospel that you might share in the glory of our Lord Jesus Christ.

What happens when you are saved? What happens when you are set apart by the Gospel message? What happens when God comes and takes up residence in your heart and soul? He begins the process of completing the work in you to conform you to the image of His Son. You begin to share in the glory of Christ Jesus and God the Father delights in that. He rejoices in the truth.

You are familiar with John 8:32 and 36. "You will know the truth and the truth will set you free. So if the Son sets you free, you will be free indeed." What does truth do? It brings freedom to the soul. The world system oppressed your soul. It kept you down. And then truth entered in. The triumph of freedom in your heart delighted God the Father. As John wrote in his third letter, "I have no greater joy than to hear that my children are walking in truth."

⸺⸺

Dear Heavenly Father,
Thank You for truth. Thank You that we
see it embodied in the person of Christ
Jesus, that in Him we see the truth about
You. We see the truth of Your love and
mercy and grace and forgiveness and
hope and life. The world wants us to see
You through different eyes. It wants us to

see You as vindictive, mean, judgmental and harsh. It suppresses the truth to trap us with evil and deception. But in Jesus we see the reality of who You are, and we thank You for that. Help us to walk in truth and experience freedom. We praise You and we thank You for truth in Christ's matchless name, Amen.

———∞∞∞———

Love Protects, Believes, Hopes, and Endures

Chapter 5

Agape love is a verb. It is an action God does on our behalf. This is really the main point of Paul's definition of love in 1 Corinthians 13. The fifteen words he used to describe love are all verbs. Many of the English translations hide this fact. For example, most of us would say that the word *patient* in verse four is an adjective. It does read "love is patient." But that is not how it reads in Greek. Patient is a present active verb. And so are the fourteen other words Paul used in this definition of love. Seven of the words show love in action. Eight show the actions love would never do.

In 1 Corinthians 13:5, Paul ties four of the "love in action" verbs together for the grand finale of his definition. Love protects, believes, hopes and endures. These four work in unison. Love protects because it believes and hopes in all things, which in turn gives it its staying power. Let's take a closer look.

Love protects. It protects us much like a storm shelter. Here in Texas, we know about storms, particularly tornadoes. When the sirens sound indicating a tornado has been sighted, everyone takes cover. For a friend of mine, this meant getting into the bath tub and covering up with a mattress. Schools, work places and homes all have rooms where people go for protection. Some people have even built storm shelters. All of these places protect those inside from the turbulent weather outside.

We know about the need for protection,

particularly as it relates to our hearts and minds. We don't like being hurt. We don't like suffering rejection, or being made fun of or used. Living in this world, however, we are all at risk. We will be hurt at some point, and the emotional pain will be such that we never want to experience it again. We've come up with all sorts of defense mechanisms to help, and we stack these psychological mattresses around us to protect us, to keep our hearts safe.

My first few years in ministry, I worked one on one with many believers. The emotional pain and heartache that I witnessed was overwhelming. I knew that I didn't want that kind of hurt in my life. I figured out that if I kept my distance from people and never let anyone get too close, I would be okay. But I wasn't okay. My defense mechanisms were limited and couldn't protect me from the feelings of loneliness and isolation. That's not the case with the love of God

God's love provides a storm shelter to guard us when the storms of life come our way. We need to be protected. Otherwise, fear, doubt and condemnation can take their toll. For each of us, life is filled with trials and tribulations. Jesus said they would come: "In the world there will be trials and tribulations" (John 16:33). But in Jesus we have someone who has overcome the world and will guard and protect us. This is His nature. Jesus Christ's protection is unlimited. Jesus is love, and love protects, always.

His love protects our hearts and minds. We will experience trials and tribulations. God's love doesn't keep those out of our lives. His love, however, keeps our hearts and minds protected. In these adverse circumstances, we can become anxious, fearful, and even confused. All of these make us vulnerable to the temptations and accusations of the world. For so long, I thought every adverse situation I experienced was God punishing me for some sin in my life. Maybe you've felt the same way. But that's not true. Jesus took the punishment for our sins, and He did so because He loved us. This love protects us from the lies and moves us to trust God to work all things together for our good.

The Greek word for *protect* or *bear* means
to "cover over in silence." In antiquity, the word
was used in the roofing industry. A roof, of
course, is a covering that protects those inside
from being vulnerable to hostile elements, the
wind, rain, and storms. That's what love does.
It provides a covering of eternal, everlasting
security. Jesus, on the cross, paid the debt of sin
for all, taking our sins forever. He took them
away, past, present, and future, so that there is
"no condemnation" for us (Romans 8:1).

We don't have to worry whether we have
stacked up enough good deeds to protect us. The
sacrifice of Jesus is permanent and has eternal
consequences. Not one thing can we add. Paul
explained it this way: "For He has rescued us
from the dominion of darkness and brought us
into the kingdom of the Son He loves, in Whom
we have redemption, the forgiveness of sins"
(Colossians 1:13,14). God's grace has placed
you into Christ. There, His love, redemption

and forgiveness protect you from all the hostile elements of the world. You can count on the fact that God would never expose your sins to the world, or open your weaknesses to the temptations of the world.

The world, on the other hand, loves to uncover sin. Once a sin is uncovered, a feeding frenzy ensues, and in minutes, often, in less than a second, everyone knows about one person's sin. The news spreads even faster when the scandal involves a pastor, or a person publicly known for his or her faith. It's just the way of the world. We Christians sit back and exclaim, "The world sure is a nasty place." We feel certain we would never expose someone's sin on social media, or blast it all over the internet and television. Now, gossip, that's another thing. Sometimes we Christians disguise our gossip with prayer chains, and we say, "Oh, did you hear about what so and so did? Please pray for him." We can't wait to pass on the information. We might even forget to pray; we just want to tell somebody else what's going on. The next person on the chain passes it to the next, and pretty soon, one person's sin is spread far and wide. But that's not love. Love protects. Love provides a covering that offers protection. That's what God does with us. Isn't that great news?

In Genesis 9 we see a picture of how love protects. After the flood, Noah planted a vineyard. He drank too much of the vineyard's wine and became drunk. Apparently, he stripped off his clothes and passed out in his tent. One of his sons, Ham, walked in and saw his father's nakedness and immediately ran out to broadcast the news to his brothers. Ham is like the world. He saw a sin and he couldn't wait to tell someone. But his brothers, Shem and Japheth, took a big robe and laid it across their shoulders. They walked into their father's tent backwards so they wouldn't see Noah, and they covered him. That's a picture of what God's love does for you and me. Do we blow it in life? Do we sin? Do we get trapped in things that we shouldn't get trapped in? Absolutely. Does God know about that? Absolutely. But does He expose it to the

world? No. He covers it. He bears it. What a
picture of love!

Peter, especially Peter, understood the love
of Jesus and how love protects. After all, it was
Peter who had declared to Jesus, "Even if I
have to die with You, I will never disown You"
(Matthew 26:33). Peter meant well, but Jesus
knew Peter just like He knows us. He knows we
will fail when we try to do things in our own
strength, especially when fear overtakes us.

Before the night was over, Peter had denied
knowing his Lord, not once, but three times. "I
don't know what you are talking about," he said
to the first person who challenged him. "I don't
know the man!" he exclaimed to the next two
challengers (26:72). Later, he recalled Jesus'
words and threw himself onto the ground. He
"wept bitterly" (26:74). Like Peter, we often
feel guilt and shame when we fail. We feel we
should be punished. But Jesus has a message for
us, a message of restoration, not condemnation.

After the resurrection, Jesus found Peter back at his old fishing job. He sought Peter out personally, not to berate him for his denial, but to restore him. Jesus looked at Peter and in a gentle spirit, simply asked, "Do you love Me?" He asked the question three times, and Peter responded, three times. Each time Jesus restored him by giving him a task. "Feed My lambs... take care of My sheep...feed My sheep" (John 21:15-17). Jesus could have pressed Peter about what he did. But that wasn't what was in Jesus' heart. He had no condemnation for Peter. Why? His loved covered. Peter's sins were taken away at the cross, covered, past, present, and future. And so were yours.

Paul tells us, "Therefore, there is no condemnation for those who are in Christ Jesus, (Romans 8:1). He goes on to say, "For what the law was powerless to do in that it was weakened by the sinful nature, God did by sending His own Son in the likeness of sinful man to be a sin offering." Where sin has been forgiven, there is no more sacrifice (Hebrews 10:18). The covering is permanent. Peter finally understood. Much later, he was able to say, "Above all, love each other deeply as children of God who belong to Christ, who belong to one another. We should love each other deeply because love covers over a multitude of sins" (1 Peter 4:8).

Love restores. It shoulders up with a person. It encourages and walks with that person and points him or her back to trusting in the love of God. Love protects. And that's true in all situations. It doesn't matter what the sin is. It doesn't matter what the need is. Love always protects. Love always believes. Love always hopes. Love always endures. That's just the definition of love. So whatever the situation is, God is never going to expose your sin to the world. He's always going to protect you because love covers a multitude of sins.

The reason that love protects is that it "believes in all things." The word *believe* comes from the Greek word that means trust or credit, to be fully persuaded about something. We hear the words *trust* and *belief* all the time. We trust in one car maker over another, one electric company over another, even one political party over another. Our trust can waver though. We trust a thing until it fails, then we move on to something else. Most of us say we trust in God. It's even written on our money. But when tragedy happens, we can doubt. That's who we are; that's our nature. But God never doubts or questions. God is love, and love believes all things, trusts all things. So what does God trust? It may seem like a strange question, but there is an answer.

God trusts the power of His love to penetrate through anything we are experiencing and bring change to our hearts and souls. Remember the thief on the cross? He surely saw Jesus look down and forgive those who crucified Him. In an instant, he recognized the voice of God, and that love penetrated his heart. At the point of his greatest pain and failure, his life was eternally changed (Luke 23:32, 42-43).

In the world, we often hear love is the answer. We hear it in songs, watch it on the movies. We get that wonderful shivery feeling like Tom Hanks and Meg Ryan had when they met on top of the Empire State Building in *Sleepless in Seattle*. But, as we all know, emotions can waver. God's love, though, never wavers. We can respond in full confidence knowing that His love is the answer to all the pains and sorrows of the human heart. His love drives out fear, bringing peace and contentment. And that's the confidence. That's what we become fully persuaded of in our relationships with one another. We can't see inside another person's heart, but we do know God's love can be trusted. We know it is the answer in all things.

Love hopes all things. The word hope is the expectation of a desire that is going to come about in our lives. But, what does God hope? God knows that His love can and does bring about a good result in our lives. His hope is rooted in the fact that He, Himself, paid the penalty for our sins, any we committed in the past and any we commit in the future. He is the sin offering that lasts throughout eternity, "…not wanting anyone to perish, but everyone to come to repentance" (2 Peter 3:9). Our human nature hopes to purchase eternal life through our good deeds, helping others, being nice, and all those types of things. But God wants us to place our hope in what He has done for us. That's what anchors us in our daily walk with the Lord. And when we are anchored in His finished work, we can reach out to others and share the gospel message, one of the greatest acts of love. We can do so with the hope that God's love will work in that person's life just as it has worked in ours.

That is why love never gives up. It perseveres and endures to the end. Do you know that God never gives up on you? Do you know that He will never turn his back on you and walk away? God sticks with you always. He perseveres, endures.

He works with us. We may get trapped in

the things of this world. But God stands with us through all of those things and continues to extend His love to us. In Hebrews 12:2, we're told to "run with perseverance the race marked out for us," to "fix our eyes on Jesus, the author and perfecter of our faith, who for the joy set before Him endured the cross, scorning its shame…"

Jesus did not stop before He completed His work. It was not until He hung on the cross that He said "It is finished" (John 19:30). He endured until the penalty demanded by sin had been paid in full. Just as He endured the cross, He is going to endure with you and me. Paul puts it this way, "…being confident of this, that He who began a good work in you will carry it on to completion until the day of Christ Jesus" (Philippians 1:6). His Spirit in us comforts our souls. As humans, we grow weary. We can lose heart, but God's love is there. And God's love can strengthen us. And God's love will strengthen us. Why? Love is an action that He takes on our behalf.

We go through trials. We go through tribulations. We go through heartaches. We suffer pain. We fight and we quarrel with each other. That's being human isn't it? It's tough. But through every trial, every tribulation, every heartache, every sorrow and pain, God endures with us. He perseveres. His love is always there and that love changes us. It develops perseverance in our hearts, so much so, that it finishes its work so that we may be mature and complete (James 1:4). We can reach out in the same way that God has reached down to us. As we will learn in the next chapter, this love never fails.

Dear Heavenly Father,

Thank You that You are love. Love just isn't one of Your many attributes, it's who You are. It's the very core of Your nature. Thank You that You loved us in the past and that You love us now, that You will continue to love us. And thank You that it's more than just a feeling You had on our behalf, but that it was and is an action. You are reaching out, knowing that Your love can bring about its desired result in our lives. You're always going to stick with us. Your love will never fail in our lives. Thank You Jesus that you love us the most. In Your matchless name. Amen.

LOVE NEVER FAILS
Chapter 6

Finally, love never fails. Isn't that great news? God's love never fails. Think about this for a moment. The verse says that love *never* fails. Never is a strong word. What it means is that not once has love ever failed, nor will it. There has never been an occasion in human history where the love of God was not without effect. Think about this as it relates to you. God's love has never been without effect in your life. That is good news, powerful news.

The word *fail* in the Greek language is a very interesting word. It literally means to fall.

It is the same word used to describe the stars falling from heaven in Mark 13:25. Love never falls away. It never fails. God never says, "I've tried love and now I'm going to plan B." Love is the only way as far as God is concerned. As Paul wrote in 1 Corinthians 12:31, love is the "most excellent way."

Many times we abandon love. We try, but love doesn't seem to be working for us or producing the results we want. So, we throw up our hands and say, "What's next?" But in reality love, God's love, is always the answer. That's why we endure. That's why we persevere. That's why we believe. That's why we protect. That's why we suffer long with others. That's why we're kind. That's why we rejoice with truth. That's why we stick with it. Love will break through. Love is always the plan. God will never fall away from loving you through thick and then. Here is the truth. Right now, at this moment, God is directing every aspect of His love toward you.

You may recall the story of Peter in prison. Luke recorded it for us in Acts 12. The church was fervently praying for his release. During the night, an angel appeared to Peter in the prison cell. He struck Peter to wake him up. When he did, the chains fell off Peter's wrists. "Fell off" is the same word Paul used to describe the idea that love never fails. Unlike the chains on Peter's wrists, God's love will never fall away from us. Paul wrote very plainly that prophesies would fail, tongues would cease and knowledge would vanish away. But not love. As the Psalmist wrote, His love endures forever.

Look back at your life. As you do, ask the Lord to show you the ways in which His love changed you. You will be amazed and awed. When you needed patience, He was patient with you. When you needed kindness, something beneficial and useful, God acted on your behalf. When the lies of the world were pressing you down, God's truth prevailed and you experienced freedom and peace in your soul. During all those painful trials and tribulations you experienced, God's protection brought you through and provided an anchor for your soul. There has never been a time in your life when God gave up on you. His love endured.

That's the power of God's love. And we are privileged people to know it, and to be convinced that nothing can separate us from His love. Paul had a moment in his life when he looked back. Romans 8:31-39 was his conclusion concerning God's love.

"What, then, shall we say in response to this? If God is for us, who can be against us? He who did not spare His own Son, but gave Him up for us all—how will He not also, along with Him, graciously give us all things? Who will bring any charge against those whom God has chosen? It is God who justifies. Who is he that condemns? Christ Jesus, who died—more than that, who was raised to life—is at the right hand of God and is also interceding for us. Who shall separate us from the love of Christ? Shall trouble or hardship or persecution or famine or nakedness or danger or sword? As it is written: "For your sake we face death all day long; we are considered as sheep to be slaughtered." No, in all these things we are more than conquerors through Him who loved us. For I am convinced that neither death nor life, neither angels nor demons, neither the present nor the future, nor any powers, neither height nor depth, nor anything else in all creation, will be able to separate us from the love of God that is in Christ Jesus our Lord."

Notice the impact of God's love on Paul. After his conversion, Paul walked through life knowing that God was for him. He lived expecting God to provide his every need. The charges levied against him by the accuser rolled off his back as he stood in the righteousness of God. He lived as a conqueror through Christ who loved him dearly. He was convinced that whatever life threw at him could not separate him from the love of God. The same can be true for you.

Paul was given a monumental task to carry

out. He lived to advance the Gospel of Jesus Christ, and he suffered mightily for the Lord. If you are like me, you stand in awe of Paul and long to meet him one day. It is easy to think that God loved him more than He loves us. But this is not true. Paul was no different than you or me. God reached down to him in the person of Jesus Christ and saved him, just like He saved you. He poured out His love on Paul, just as He has poured out His love on you and is doing so as you read these words. Like Paul, you can walk confidently through life knowing that you are loved by God.

God, however, never intended us to be merely recipients of His love. Love thinks of others. "God so loved the world that He gave…" This is the first verse most of us memorized. Here is the exciting news of the Gospel. Jesus' love now resides in your heart. Paul put it this way; "God has poured out his love into our hearts through the Holy Spirit…" (Romans 5:5) This love is not content to sit idly by. It is looking for a way to flow out of you into the life of someone else. He wants to use you to pass His love on to others. This just makes since doesn't it? "Since God so loved us," John wrote, "we also ought to love one another" (1 John 4:11).

Notice how John began, "Since God so loved us." That is the most important part. The world stands against us, but not God. The Bible is clear. He loves us without strings attached. All He asks of us is to remain in His love. This is the key to loving others. Jesus illustrated it this way: "I am the vine; you are the branches. If a man remains in Me, and I in him, he will bear much fruit…" (John 15:5). The fruit we bear is love. Bearing this fruit has enormous implications for us.

"How can I know for sure that I am really saved?" Maybe you have asked this question. For the last several years, callers to our radio broadcast have asked this more than any other question. Loving others is one way that God assures our hearts that we truly belong to Him. Many of the believers John wrote to struggled with this question. They weren't sure of their salvation. Strange doctrines had reached their ears causing them great confusion. John cut straight through the clutter: "Everyone who loves has been born of God and knows God" (1 John 4:7). You can't pass on the love of God unless you have been born again and know God. Loving others is proof that you belong to Him.

How would you defend the Gospel? What answer would you give for the hope that is within you? A whole branch of theology called apologetics was developed to help answer these questions. Are you picturing right now a debate between a Christian and an atheist? That is the image apologetics brings to my mind. Certainly, there is an abundance of evidence, hard core facts that make a solid case for the Christian faith. But there is something that is even more convincing, and far more powerful. Jesus spoke of this to His disciples the night before He was crucified. "A new command I give you: Love one another. As I have loved you, so must you love one another. By this all men will know that

you are my disciples, if you love one another"
(John 13:33, 34). Loving others is evidence that
the Gospel is true.

For some perspective, let's take a journey
back to the first century, around 35 A.D. The
church had just begun. The first members were
all Jewish. They shared a common history and
culture. And now they shared Christ. Love was
easy for them. But God loved the world, not just
the nation of Israel. Salvation was for whoever
called upon the name of the Lord, even the Gentiles and the Samaritans.

God made this clear to Peter in a vision. In
the vision, Peter heard a voice say, "Do not call
anything impure that God has made clean" (Acts
10:15). When the vision ended, the Spirit told
Peter three men were looking for him and not
to hesitate to go with them. When they arrived,
Peter went with them to Caesarea to the home
of Cornelius, a Roman centurion. Peter entered
the home and began to tell the Gentile crowd
that had gathered there about Jesus Christ. God

poured out His Spirit on them just as He had done with the Jews on the Day of Pentecost. Cornelius, along with his family and friends were saved and added to the church. Jew and Gentile, now one in Christ.

Here is what happened. The Gospel message turned people who hated each other into brothers and sisters in Christ. Not an ounce of love had ever flowed between these two groups. Only hatred and animosity. But now, the Lord moved in their hearts to love one another. Jews loving Gentiles. Gentiles loving Jews. The world looked on and the evidence was overwhelming. Those people were truly disciples of Jesus Christ. Our love for one another offers the same powerful evidence today.

As I learned on my Six Flags adventure with Floyd, the love of God is not something we can produce through human effort. We just don't have it in us. Jesus made this point abundantly clear. "Apart from Me, you can do nothing." Love does not originate with us. God is the source. He is love. Only as we abide in Him, like a branch abiding in the vine, will His love flow through us. What happens when a branch is cut off from the vine? It withers and dies. Don't expect to gather any fruit from that old dead branch. When it is attached to vine, however, that same branch offers fruit in abundance. As believers, we are attached to the vine, and nothing can separate us from Him. We will never be cut off. His life flows through us producing the fruit of love in us. It is mind-boggling when you think about it. The same love He directed toward you can now flow through you into the life of another person.

This is the greatest joy you can experience and it fulfills your highest calling. Paul made this statement in his letter to the Galatians: "The only thing that counts is faith expressing itself through love" (Galatians 5:6). This is Paul's explanation of the vine and branch illustration. Our faith in Jesus Christ is expressed in love to others. This is what counts, nothing else. John gave us these commands: "Believe in the name of His Son, Jesus Christ, and love one another as He commanded us" (1 John 3:23). This is the Christian life. All of these passages lead to this staggering truth: God uses us to show the world what love is.

Have you come to know and rely on the love of God? He demonstrated this love in vivid detail through Christ's death on the cross. It is "not that we loved God, but that He loved us and sent His Son as the propitiation for our sins" (1 John 4:10). In Christ, you stand before God as a forgiven person. Your sins have been taken away once and for all. You may be worried that someday God is going to punish you for your sins. Let the love of God cast that fear aside. Jesus died in your place. He took the punishment you deserved. That's love. That same love He demonstrated on Calvary's hill is present right now. Abide in it. Rely on it. It never fails.

Dear Heavenly Father,
Thank you for loving me. I want to
continue to grow in Your love. I want
to love others as You have loved me.
Keep me dependent upon You, trusting
in You alone to produce Your love in me.
I pray as Paul did that Your Spirit will
strengthen me with power so that I can
grasp the height, the depth, the length,
and the breadth of the love of Christ and
to know this love that surpasses knowl-
edge. Thank You that You always do
immeasurably more than I ask or imag-
ine. Thank You for using me to show the
world what love is. In Jesus' loving and
matchless name. Amen.

Acknowledgments

A special thank you goes to Martha Moore for her help with the manuscript. She made the book better. Also, thanks goes to Vivian Foster, Kim Groff, Jeannie Thompson and Greg Parke for their great work on this project.

I would also like to acknowledge Spiro Zodhiates for his works, *The Complete Word Study New Testament* and *The Complete Word Study Dictionary New Testament.* Both have been invaluable tools to me in my study of the Bible, and were extremely helpful in broadening my understanding of the love of God.

About Bob

 Bob is the CEO of Basic Gospel. Bob can be heard on the live, call-in radio broadcast Basic Gospel, on air each weekday at 3:00 & 3:30 P.M. central time on stations across the country as well as *BasicGospel.net.* Each day, Bob addresses life issues with Biblical truth in his own practical, compassionate, down-to-earth style.

Follow Bob on

- Twitter @RCChristopherJr
- Facebook at fb.com/BasicGospel
- Read his blog at FirstLifeThenChange.com

About Basic Gospel

Hear it. Believe it. Live it.

The Gospel of Jesus Christ is simple, powerful, and life changing. It declares the love of God for mankind. It is the good news people long to hear. Radio delivers it straight to the heart.

But it is not enough just to hear the good news. God wants to make His love a reality in our lives. He wants us to believe it and live it.

At Basic Gospel, we are dedicated to proclaiming the name of Jesus Christ and the profound simplicity of His love and grace.

Our hope is that the clear presentation of the Basic Gospel and the singular focus on the death, burial and resurrection of Jesus Christ will anchor listeners to the love of God and will encourage them to experience the fullness of the New Covenant life that is theirs in Christ.

BASICGOSPEL.NET

Made in the USA
San Bernardino, CA
15 March 2014